Connections!

EARTH

CAROLINE GRIMSHAW

TEXT **IQBAL HUSSAIN**

SCIENCE CONSULTANT **JOHN STRINGER**

ENVIRONMENTAL CONSULTANT **FELIX DODDS**
UNITED NATIONS ENVIRONMENT & DEVELOPMENT – UK COMMITTEE
COORDINATOR

ILLUSTRATIONS **NICK DUFFY** ☆ **SPIKE GERRELL** ☆ **JO MOORE**

A TWO-CAN BOOK
PUBLISHED BY
THOMSON LEARNING
NEW YORK

Connections!
EARTH

CREATIVE AND EDITORIAL DIRECTOR
CONCEPT/FORMAT/DESIGN
CAROLINE GRIMSHAW

TEXT **IQBAL HUSSAIN**

SCIENCE CONSULTANT **JOHN STRINGER**

ENVIRONMENTAL CONSULTANT **FELIX DODDS**
UNITED NATIONS ENVIRONMENT
& DEVELOPMENT – UK COMMITTEE COORDINATOR

ILLUSTRATIONS
NICK DUFFY ☆ SPIKE GERRELL ☆ JO MOORE

THANKS TO
DEBBIE DORMAN PICTURE RESEARCH
JUSTINE COOPER AND ROBERT SVED EDITORIAL SUPPORT
AND ANDREW JARVIS ☆ RUTH KING
CHARLES SHAAR MURRAY ☆ PAUL DU NOYER

BOOKS IN THIS SERIES

PEOPLE BUILDINGS EARTH

PUBLISHED IN 1995 BY TWO-CAN PUBLISHING LTD
IN ASSOCIATION WITH THOMSON LEARNING, NEW YORK.
COPYRIGHT © TWO-CAN PUBLISHING LTD, 1995.
PRINTED AND BOUND IN BELGIUM BY PROOST NV

LIBRARY OF CONGRESS CATALOGING-IN-PUBLICATION DATA
GRIMSHAW, CAROLINE.
  EARTH / CAROLINE GRIMSHAW [CREATIVE AND EDITORIAL DIRECTOR] ; TEXT, IQBAL HUSSAIN ;
ILLUSTRATIONS, NICK DUFFY, SPIKE GERRELL, JO MOORE.
  P. CM. — (CONNECTIONS!) INCLUDES INDEX.
  ISBN 1-56847-453-9
  1. EARTH—MISCELLANEA—JUVENILE LITERATURE. 2. CHILDREN'S QUESTIONS AND ANSWERS.
[1. EARTH—MISCELLANEA. 2. QUESTIONS AND ANSWERS.] I. HUSSAIN, IQBAL, 1971– II. DUFFY,
NICK, ILL. III. GERRELL, SPIKE, ILL. IV. MOORE, JO, ILL. V. TITLE. VI. SERIES: CONNECTIONS!
(THOMSON LEARNING (FIRM)
QB631.4.G75 1995
550—DC20   95-6702

Contents

DISCOVER THE CONNECTIONS THROUGH QUESTIONS AND ANSWERS...
YOU CAN READ THIS BOOK FROM START TO FINISH OR
LEAPFROG THROUGH THE SECTIONS
FOLLOWING THE PATHS SUGGESTED
IN THESE SPECIAL "CONNECT! BOXES."

Connect!

ENJOY YOUR JOURNEY OF
DISCOVERY AND UNDERSTANDING

It's time to make sense of the

mysterious planet

Where did Earth come from?

What is the planet made of?

Why does Earth look like it does?

You'll find all these questions
(and more!) answered in PART ONE of your journey of
discovery and understanding. Turn the page! - - - >

1 Where did the planet come from?

No one knows for sure.

The birth of Earth

Many religions, such as Christianity, Judaism, and Islam, describe the power of God behind the origins of Earth. Other religions, such as Buddhism, have creation stories and legends.

⬆ This is a statue of Buddha. Buddhism is based on the teachings of an Indian prince, Siddhartha Gautama.

⬆ Christian followers of Jesus Christ – a Jew who lived in Palestine nearly two thousand years ago – believe he is God's son.

Scientists think that Earth was formed naturally from a swirling cloud of dust and gases.

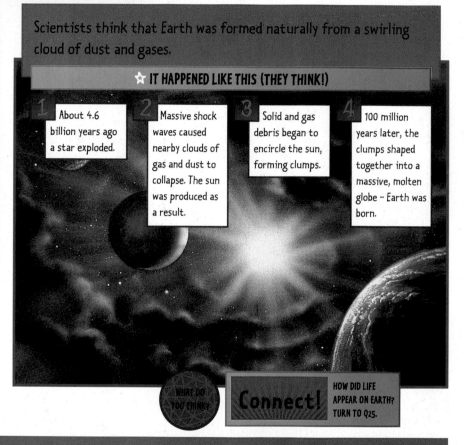

☆ IT HAPPENED LIKE THIS (THEY THINK!)

1 About 4.6 billion years ago a star exploded.

2 Massive shock waves caused nearby clouds of gas and dust to collapse. The sun was produced as a result.

3 Solid and gas debris began to encircle the sun, forming clumps.

4 100 million years later, the clumps shaped together into a massive, molten globe – Earth was born.

WHAT DO YOU THINK?

Connect!

HOW DID LIFE APPEAR ON EARTH? TURN TO Q25.

2 Is Earth the only planet?

No! In our solar system, it is one of at least nine planets orbiting the sun.

PLANET	DIAMETER
MERCURY	3,031 MI
VENUS	7,521 MI
EARTH	7,927 MI
MARS	4,217 MI
JUPITER	88,850 MI
SATURN	74,901 MI
URANUS	31,765 MI
NEPTUNE	30,777 MI
PLUTO	1,429 MI

EARTH = fifth largest planet in the solar system.

SOLAR SYSTEM = part of the Milky Way, consisting of the nine planets and the sun.

MILKY WAY = part of a galaxy, made up of millions of stars and planets.

GALAXY = collection of about 100 billion stars and planets. There are at least 6 billion galaxies.

☆ OUR SUN IS JUST ONE OF BILLIONS OF STARS.

What is the planet made of?

Rather like an onion, the inside of Earth has a number of layers. They are made of rock and cover a solid iron and nickel core. There are four main layers.

1 Crust

This is the surface layer of rock. It varies in thickness from 4 mi underneath the oceans to 22 mi beneath the continents.

2 Mantle

About 1,800 mi thick, this is solid rock near the top, but it becomes molten deeper down.

3 Outer core

Made of liquid iron and nickel, this layer is 1,240 mi thick.

4 Inner core

This is believed to be a solid iron and nickel sphere. It is 1,700 mi across and has an estimated temperature of 8100°F.

The outside of the planet is surrounded by a layer of gases, called the atmosphere.

Connect!
BUT WHAT MAKES THE PLANET LOOK LIKE IT DOES? FIND OUT IN Q7.

Connect!
WHY IS THE ATMOSPHERE CRUCIAL TO LIFE? Q28 HAS THE ANSWER.

Question 4 How much does the planet weigh?

A staggering **6 sextillion tons**! What's more, it's getting heavier, as each year it picks up dust from space.

Question 5 How old is the planet?

About **4.6 billion years** old.

AND HOW DO WE KNOW THIS?
Scientists looked at meteorite samples and pieces of moon rock, which were created at the same time as Earth. By seeing how much radiation the rocks and meteorites gave off, scientists worked out their age. Both are 4.6 billion years old, which must also be the age of Earth.

Question 6 And how wide is it?

Earth is not a perfect sphere, but is very slightly pear-shaped. It's squashed at the poles and bulges at the equator around the middle.

AND HOW DO WE KNOW THIS?
BY MEASURING THE CIRCUMFERENCE (THE CIRCULAR DISTANCE) OF EARTH AROUND THE POLES AND AROUND THE EQUATOR. IF EARTH WAS A PERFECT SPHERE THESE TWO FIGURES WOULD BE THE SAME.

MEASURING THE CIRCUMFERENCE AROUND THE POLES = 24,856 MI

MEASURING THE CIRCUMFERENCE AROUND THE EQUATOR = 24,903 MI

Connect!
HOW DID WE DISCOVER THE EARTH WAS NOT FLAT? TURN TO Q31.

☆ IT WOULD TAKE A TOP ATHLETE A MONTH AND A HALF TO SPRINT NONSTOP AROUND THE WORLD!

Why does the land look like it does?

It has a lot to do with a process called plate tectonics.

Geysers

Geysers are found only in areas where volcanoes are active. The boiling jet of steam and water shoots out of the ground because of growing pressure down below.

⬆ Old Faithful in Yellowstone Park spouts about 10,000 gallons of water every 30–90 minutes, reaching heights of over 160 ft.

Connect!

HOW CAN WATER PROVIDE US WITH ENERGY? TURN TO Q42.

Earthquakes

Earthquakes occur along the edges of tectonic plates. Two passing plates suddenly slip, releasing a tremendous amount of energy and causing dramatic ground movement. There are around half a million earthquakes each year, but only about a thousand cause any serious damage.

CASE STUDY Japan

DATE	JANUARY 17, 1995.
RANGE	CAUSED DAMAGE OVER AN AREA OF 13,900 SQ MI.
DAMAGE	THOUSANDS OF HOMES WERE DESTROYED BY THE QUAKE AND RESULTING FIRES. HIGHWAYS AND RAILROADS COLLAPSED, KILLING MORE THAN 4,000 PEOPLE.

Tectonic plates

Earth's outer shell, or crust, is not one smooth piece as you might imagine. It is actually made up of several vast slabs of rock, called tectonic plates. These fit together like a jigsaw puzzle. The pressure caused by two plates meeting or sliding past each other makes the land buckle, bend, or pull apart. As a result, **volcanoes**, **mountains**, **earthquakes**, and **geysers** occur at plate boundaries.

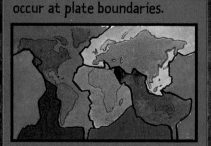

⬆ Earth is constantly changing. Tectonic plates move between .39 in. and 6 in. a year, carrying with them the continents and oceans lying on top.

Connect!

HOW WILL PLATE TECTONICS AFFECT THE WAY THE WORLD LOOKS IN THE FUTURE? TURN TO Q19.

Mountains

Mountains cover about a quarter of Earth's surface. They are formed when two tectonic plates smash into each other. The force causes the land to crumple and fold upward.

THE ROCKY MOUNTAINS	
LOCATION	NORTH AMERICA, FROM ALASKA TO NEW MEXICO.
AGE	70 MILLION YEARS.
HEIGHT	BETWEEN 980 FT AND 14,440 FT.
LENGTH	OVER 3,745 MI.
SHAPE	FROM PEAKS AND PINNACLES TO FLAT TOPS AND PLATEAUS.

Volcanoes

Volcanoes are found in places where Earth's crust is weak. This tends to be near the boundaries of continental plates. Molten rock, or magma, is forced out of cracks in the surface by the pressure from underground gases. The shape of the volcano depends on the type of lava and the force of the eruption.

SHIELD Gentle slopes

CINDER CONE Steep slopes

STRATA Cone-shaped

QUESTION 8

How much of the planet is covered by water?

Almost three-quarters! Water covers about 142 million sq mi, or 71%, of Earth's surface.

QUESTION 9

Where do you find salt water and freshwater?

96.5%
OF THE PLANET'S WATER = **SALT WATER**
(FOUND IN SEAS AND OCEANS)

THE PACIFIC OCEAN IS THE LARGEST STRETCH OF WATER, COVERING ALMOST ONE-THIRD OF THE PLANET.

3.5%
OF THE PLANET'S WATER = **FRESHWATER**

★ **WHERE IS FRESHWATER STORED?**

| ICE SHEETS, GLACIERS, AND SNOW – **69%** | UNDERGROUND IN ROCKS – **30.7%** | LAKES – **0.25%** | ATMOSPHERE – **0.04%** | RIVERS – **0.010%** |

QUESTION 10

How deep is the deepest ocean?

The Marianas Trench in the Pacific Ocean is the deepest place on the planet. Its depth of 36,161 ft is enough to completely cover Mount Everest.

HAS ANYONE BEEN DOWN THERE?
ALMOST. THE U.S. NAVY'S DEEP SEA VESSEL TRIESTE MANAGED TO DESCEND TO A DEPTH OF 35,813 FT.

QUESTION 11

Are oceans always cold?

No! In 1977, scientists discovered hot water gushing out from cracks in the Pacific Ocean sea-bed. The water around these cracks, or hydrothermal vents, reaches temperatures of over 570°F.

EXAMINE THIS FOOD CYCLE

Vent gives off sulfur – poisonous to most animals. → Bacteria feed off sulfur. ↓ Giant tube worms called Riftia feed off bacteria. → Creatures such as white crabs feed off worms. ←

QUESTION 12

What causes tides?

The moon exerts a force called gravity on the oceans. The water is pulled into a bulge toward the moon, creating a high tide. A similar bulge appears on the other side of the world. The two bulges follow the moon as it circles Earth, resulting in a cycle of low and high tides.

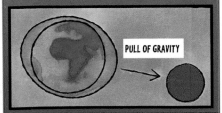

PULL OF GRAVITY

QUESTION 13

Why is seawater salty?

As rivers make their way down to the sea, they flow over many rocky landscapes. Rocks contain minerals, including salt. The river water washes away some of the salt and carries it along and out to sea.

Connect!

HOW DOES WATER CHANGE THE LANDSCAPE? FIND OUT IN Q20.

Prove It!

Freezing seawater helps get rid of most of the salt in it. Prove it by making an ice cube from clean, salty water and then licking it.

QUESTION

14 Why are some places hot and some places not?

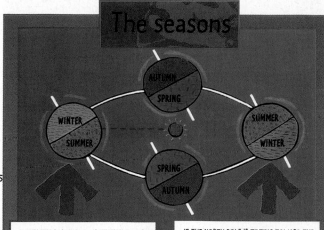

1 The nearer the equator you are the hotter it is, as the sun's heat strikes the planet directly around the equator, but obliquely nearer the poles.

2 Away from the equator there is less sunshine, so the temperature drops and it is colder.

3 It is warmer in big towns and cities because heat is trapped by the blanket of pollution in the air.

4 As air rises it expands and its temperature falls. This is why mountain air is cooler than air in flat areas.

5 Large stretches of water store the sun's heat. Coastal areas are heated by the warm ocean breezes, making them milder than places inland.

The seasons

WHEN THE SOUTH POLE IS TILTING TOWARD THE SUN, IT IS SUMMER IN THE SOUTHERN HEMISPHERE AND WINTER IN THE NORTH.

IF THE NORTH POLE IS TILTING TOWARD THE SUN, IT IS SUMMER IN THE NORTHERN HEMISPHERE AND WINTER IN THE SOUTH.

The seasons also have an effect on the temperature. As Earth spins on its axis, it tilts slightly. During Earth's journey around the sun, this tilt affects the amount of sunshine and heat the planet's two halves, or hemispheres, receive.

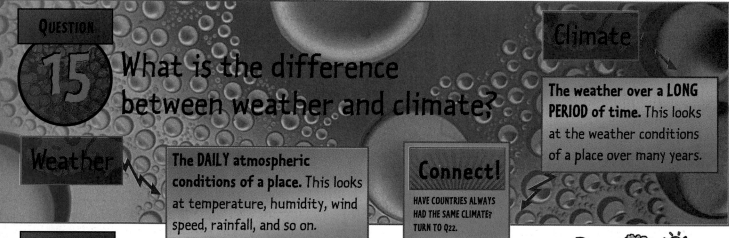

QUESTION

15 What is the difference between weather and climate?

Climate

The weather over a LONG PERIOD of time. This looks at the weather conditions of a place over many years.

Weather

The DAILY atmospheric conditions of a place. This looks at temperature, humidity, wind speed, rainfall, and so on.

Connect!

HAVE COUNTRIES ALWAYS HAD THE SAME CLIMATE? TURN TO Q22.

QUESTION

16 Can weather be dangerous? Yes

Weather conditions can wreak devastation on a major scale.

☆ STORMY WEATHER

HURRICANES, TYPHOONS, AND CYCLONES ARE DIFFERENT NAMES FOR SIMILAR POWERFUL STORMS. THE WHIRLING MASSES OF CLOUD, WIND, AND RAIN CAN REACH SPEEDS OF OVER 220 MI PER HOUR. IN 1970, A CYCLONE HIT THE GANGES DELTA, IN BANGLADESH, KILLING A MILLION PEOPLE.

☆ TOO MUCH RAIN

TOO MUCH WATER CAN BE A BAD THING. HEAVY RAINFALL CAUSES RIVERS TO SWELL AND OVERFLOW. SINCE 600 B.C., CHINA'S HUANG RIVER HAS FLOODED MORE THAN 1,500 TIMES. IN SEPTEMBER 1887, IT BURST ITS BANKS IN A DEVASTATING FLOOD THAT KILLED 900,000 PEOPLE.

☆ DROUGHT

PROBLEMS ON THE PLANET CAN BE CAUSED WHEN THERE IS NOT ENOUGH RAINFALL. THIS IS CALLED A DROUGHT. PLANTS CANNOT GROW IN THE DRY EARTH AND THE GROUND BECOMES CRACKED AND PARCHED. THE DRIEST PLACE ON EARTH IS THE ATACAMA DESERT, IN CHILE. UNTIL A FREAK FLOOD IN 1971, THERE HAD BEEN NO RAINFALL THERE FOR ALMOST 400 YEARS.

Connect!

CHECK OUT Q21 TO SEE SOME REALLY STRANGE LANDFORMS FASHIONED BY THE WEATHER.

Here's your chance to discover the secrets behind the

changing planet

Have continents always had the same climates?

The weather...

how does it affect the way the land looks?

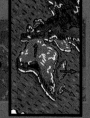

What will the planet look like in 50 million years' time?

The journey continues. Just turn the page and you will find out in PART TWO that nothing stands still!

Questions

20 What else changes the way the planet looks?

Earth's mountains, rocks, hills, and valleys might look solid in shape and structure, but they are not. They are constantly being changed and worn away by two processes – weathering and erosion.

Weathering ➡ WEATHERING IS WHEN ROCKS ARE BROKEN DOWN BY THE ACTION OF THE WEATHER.

There are two main weathering actions.

1

PHYSICAL WEATHERING BREAKS DOWN ROCKS INTO SMALLER PIECES. HERE ARE TWO WAYS IN WHICH PHYSICAL WEATHERING MIGHT HAPPEN:

● On a warm day the sun heats up the rock, making it expand slightly. As it cools in the evening, the rock shrinks, or contracts. This causes pressure inside the stone. Cracks appear and eventually bits of the rock start falling off.

● In colder weather, the rock is broken down by a process known as both the ice wedge and freeze-thaw:

⬆ RAINWATER ENTERS CRACKS IN THE ROCK.

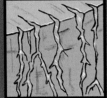

⬆ IT FREEZES AND EXPANDS, FORCING THE CRACKS WIDER APART. AS THE TEMPERATURE RISES AND FALLS, SO THE WATER MELTS AND FREEZES.

⬆ THIS FREEZE-THAW ACTION EVENTUALLY MAKES BITS OF THE ROCK DROP OFF.

Prove It!

2

CHEMICAL WEATHERING DESTROYS ROCKS BY A CHEMICAL PROCESS.

⬆ Water containing limestone often forms spectacular stalactites.

Limestone is particularly prone to chemical weathering caused by rain. Carbon dioxide gas in raindrops attacks the limestone and dissolves it.

Connect!

READ Q22 TO FIND OUT IF CONTINENTS HAVE ALWAYS HAD THE SAME CLIMATES THAT EXIST TODAY.

WHAT ELSE CAN CAUSE WEATHERING?

Animals and plants also play their part in weathering.

TREE ROOTS ENTER CRACKS IN ROCKS AND PULL THEM APART.

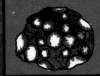

MOSSES AND LICHENS SOMETIMES PRODUCE WEAK ACIDS THAT WEAR AWAY AT THE ROCK SURFACE.

ANIMALS SUCH AS MOLES AND RABBITS LOOSEN THE GROUND AROUND WEATHERED ROCKS. THIS LETS WATER SEEP IN.

EROSION

WHAT HAPPENS NEXT?

EROSION IS THE MOVEMENT OF THE FRAGMENTS – OR DEBRIS – PRODUCED BY WEATHERING AND THEIR EFFECT ON THE LANDSCAPE. THE ROCK PIECES ARE PICKED UP BY THE WIND, WATER, AND ICE. AS THE FRAGMENTS ARE CARRIED ALONG, THEY SMASH AND GRIND AGAINST THE SURROUNDING ROCKS.

1. The shape of the land is slowly altered, or eroded, by the fragments.
2. The debris becomes smaller and smaller and is finally deposited in a different place.

Connect! HOW CAN WE MAKE USE OF THE WIND AND WATER AS POWERFUL ENERGY SOURCES? SEE Q42.

RIVER EROSION – THE DEBRIS THAT IS CARRIED IN THE WATER ERODES THE RIVER BANKS.

ICE EROSION – GLACIERS CONTAINING DEBRIS ERODE ROCK BY SCRAPING PAST IT.

WIND EROSION – THE WIND ERODES ROCK BY PICKING UP AND FLINGING DEBRIS AT IT.

RAINWATER EROSION – FALLING RAINDROPS CREATE DENTS IN THE ROCK. THIS IS A VERY SLOW PROCESS.

SEA EROSION – WAVES CARRYING PEBBLES AND SAND ERODE THE CLIFFS WITH THEIR POUNDING ACTION.

QUESTION 21

Can weather conditions create weird landforms?

The effects of weathering and erosion can result in strange-looking natural structures.

Connect! HOW HAVE HUMANS CHANGED THE WAY THE PLANET LOOKS? TURN TO Q33.

THE MITTENS, MONUMENT VALLEY, UTAH – WATER AND WIND EROSION.

ROCK PILLARS, NEGEV DESERT, ISRAEL – WEATHERING AND WIND EROSION.

WAVE ROCK, PERTH, AUSTRALIA – WEATHERING.

HOODOOS, ROCKY MOUNTAINS, CANADA – FLASH FLOOD AND WIND EROSION.

QUESTION

22 Have continents always had the same climates?

Earth's climate is forever changing. Hot places, such as deserts, have been freezing cold in the past. Similarly, some of today's cold areas once experienced sweltering climates.

HOW HAS THE WORLD'S CLIMATE CHANGED?

1,000 YEARS AGO	5,000 YEARS AGO	18,000 YEARS AGO	50 MILLION YEARS AGO	450 MILLION YEARS AGO
GREENLAND WAS WARM ENOUGH TO REAR SHEEP, CATTLE, AND PIGS.	THE SAHARA DESERT WAS GREEN AND LUSH. LIONS AND ELEPHANTS WANDERED ACROSS IT.	THE TOP HALF OF NORTH AMERICA LAY UNDER AN ICE SHEET OVER 800 FT THICK.	LONDON'S TROPICAL CLIMATE MEANT THE CITY WAS COVERED WITH CROCODILE-INFESTED SWAMPS.	THE SAHARA DESERT WAS A BLEAK WASTELAND, TOTALLY COVERED WITH ICE.

How does the climate change?

The world's climate seems to change in a regular pattern. Short warm periods, called interglacials, are followed by long cold periods, or glacials. Luckily for us, we are living in an interglacial period. However, some scientists believe the next Ice Age will strike in a thousand years.

Connect! TURN TO Q30 TO DISCOVER HOW WE KNOW SO MUCH ABOUT PAST CLIMATES.

Why does the climate change?

THERE ARE TWO MAIN THEORIES:

1. Tectonic plate action means continents are forever changing their positions. Plates drifting toward the poles means that land receives colder weather, while those moving nearer the equator means that land will have hotter weather.

2. Ice Ages may be caused by a slight wobble of Earth as it orbits the sun. The wobble happens about once every 96,000 years. The small movement dramatically affects the amount of heat reaching Earth.

QUESTION

23 How do climates divide the world?

The world is split into six major climatic regions.

TEMPERATE WARM SUMMER, MILD WINTER, CAN RAIN AT ANY TIME. TEMPERATURE: 21°F TO 77°F.

POLAR VERY COLD, DRY, WINDY, LAND AND SEA COVERED BY ICE. TEMPERATURE: −120°F TO 50°F.

TUNDRA COLD, WINDY, LITTLE RAINFALL. TEMPERATURE: −22°F TO 63°F.

TROPICAL ALWAYS HOT, ALTERNATE DRY AND RAINY SEASONS. TEMPERATURE: 70°F TO 86°F.

EQUATORIAL ALWAYS HOT, DAILY RAINFALL, NO SEASONAL CHANGE. TEMPERATURE: 81°F TO 82°F.

DESERT VERY HOT DAYS, COOL NIGHTS, WINDY, LITTLE RAINFALL. TEMPERATURE: 10°F TO 136°F.

Connect! WHAT MIGHT HAPPEN TO THE EARTH'S CLIMATE IN THE FUTURE? TURN TO Q45.

All you ever needed to know about

life

on Earth

How does the planet support life?

What is life?

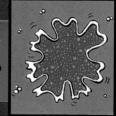

How has life on Earth changed since the beginning of time?

Read all about life on
Earth in PART THREE of your journey.
Just turn the page! - - - ✈

QUESTION **24**

What is life?

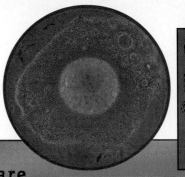

Almost all living things on the planet are made of cells. These are the smallest units of life. Cells carry out a number of functions that allow the process of life to exist.

↑ An amoeba is a tiny creature that only has one cell.

↑ Humans are made up of more than 50 billion cells.

How is living matter organized?

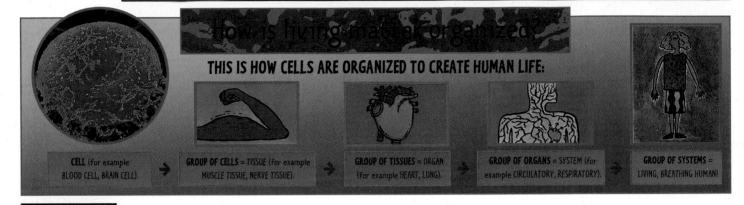

THIS IS HOW CELLS ARE ORGANIZED TO CREATE HUMAN LIFE:

| CELL (for example BLOOD CELL, BRAIN CELL). | → | GROUP OF CELLS = TISSUE (for example MUSCLE TISSUE, NERVE TISSUE). | → | GROUP OF TISSUES = ORGAN (for example HEART, LUNG). | → | GROUP OF ORGANS = SYSTEM (for example CIRCULATORY, RESPIRATORY). | → | GROUP OF SYSTEMS = LIVING, BREATHING HUMAN! |

QUESTION **25**

Why did living things suddenly appear on Earth?

THE TWO MAIN **Theories**

1 **CREATION STORIES** Many religions have stories to explain the origins of life.

2 **SCIENTIFIC EXPLANATION** Life arose on the planet from a chain of natural events.

When Earth was formed 4.6 billion years ago, it was too hot to support any life. Gradually, the planet cooled down. The first signs of life appeared in the water over 1 billion years later.

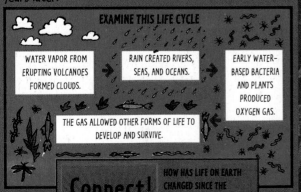

EXAMINE THIS LIFE CYCLE

WATER VAPOR FROM ERUPTING VOLCANOES FORMED CLOUDS.

RAIN CREATED RIVERS, SEAS, AND OCEANS.

EARLY WATER-BASED BACTERIA AND PLANTS PRODUCED OXYGEN GAS.

THE GAS ALLOWED OTHER FORMS OF LIFE TO DEVELOP AND SURVIVE.

Connect! HOW HAS LIFE ON EARTH CHANGED SINCE THE BEGINNING OF TIME? SEE Q29.

☆ **BUT WHERE DID THE BACTERIA AND PLANTS APPEAR FROM?**

A series of random chemical reactions acted on the chemicals already in the oceans and air. The reactions were probably set off by energy from a powerful natural source, such as lightning. The chemicals joined into simple structures and gradually became more complex. Eventually, after millions of years, they developed into the first living organisms.

IN 1953, AMERICAN SCIENTISTS UREY AND MILLER CARRIED OUT AN EXPERIMENT TO DEMONSTRATE THIS.

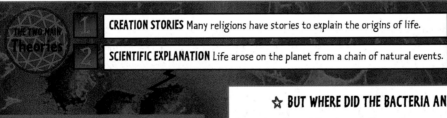

ELECTRODE (REPRESENTING THE LIGHTNING) PROVIDES THE ENERGY TO MAKE THE CHEMICALS REACT.

ELECTRODE

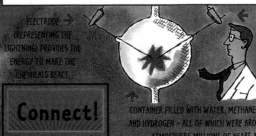

Connect! HOW HAVE WE CHANGED THE PLANET IN ORDER TO SURVIVE? TURN TO Q33.

CONTAINER FILLED WITH WATER, METHANE, AMMONIA, AND HYDROGEN – ALL OF WHICH WERE AROUND IN THE ATMOSPHERE MILLIONS OF YEARS AGO.

RESULT – THE REACTIONS CREATED VARIOUS COMPLEX SUBSTANCES SUCH AS AMINO ACIDS. ALL LIVING THINGS ARE MADE OF THESE CHEMICAL STRUCTURES. WAS THIS HOW LIFE BEGAN?

26 Is Earth the only planet with life on it?

Earth's position in relation to the sun means it can support living organisms. It is not too hot, like Mercury, or too cold, like Pluto. No other planets in our solar system have life on them.

How do we know?

Space probes have taken pictures and measurements of the planets, but none have found evidence of extra-terrestrial life.

Mariner 10 (1973) Pictures of Mercury.

Viking 1 (1975) Data on Mars.

Voyager 2 (1977) Flies past Jupiter, Saturn, Uranus, and Neptune.

Venera 13 (1981) Venus soil analyzed.

But there are billions of stars and planets in the universe. At least a million could have similar conditions to Earth and be able to produce life. There may be living organisms somewhere out there – we just haven't found them yet.

Connect! WHAT DO YOU NEED TO SURVIVE ON A PLANET? CHECK OUT Q28.

27 How does the planet affect what plants and animals look like?

The Earth's many different climates and landscapes are always changing. To survive, plants and animals have adapted to cope with new conditions. This process of gradual change is called **evolution**. Here are some good examples.

The **POLAR BEAR** has thick, shaggy fur to keep out the cold.

The **MOLE** has broad front feet for digging underground.

The **GIRAFFE** has a long neck for reaching high leaves.

The **CACTUS** has prickles to stop it being eaten.

☆ WHO FIRST THOUGHT OF EVOLUTION?

Charles Darwin. In 1859, he explained his ideas in his book, On The Origin Of Species. His main theory was called natural selection, or the "survival of the fittest." This says that only the most healthy, well-adapted plants and animals ultimately survive.

THIS IS HOW NATURAL SELECTION WORKS:

1. Suppose one gazelle in a group has longer legs than the others.
2. This means it can move fast enough to outrun predators.
3. Most of the shorter-legged gazelles are caught and killed.
4. The long-legged gazelle survives and breeds.
5. Some of its offspring are also born with long legs.
6. In time, most of the gazelles end up with long legs because that increases their chances of survival.

Connect! HOW WILL THE CHANGING ENVIRONMENT AFFECT FUTURE EVOLUTION? FIND OUT IN Q41.

QUESTION

28 If you were making a new planet, what would be on your shopping list for survival?

 **YOU NEED AIR TO BREATHE**

Connect! WHAT HAPPENS WHEN AIR IS IMPURE? FIND OUT IN Q39.

Almost all living things need air to survive. Earth is surrounded by a warm layer of air called the atmosphere. The atmosphere allows just enough of the sun's heat to enter the planet without making it too cold or too hot. It also stops heat escaping into space.

Which gases make up the air?

The air is made up of a number of gases, but oxygen and nitrogen are the main ones.

■	**NITROGEN** = 78%
■	**OXYGEN** = 21%
■	**ARGON** = 0.9%
■	**CARBON DIOXIDE** = 0.03%
■	**OTHER GASES** = 0.07%

How does air support life?

Plants and animals use air, helping to maintain the balance of gases in the air in the following way.

HUMANS AND OTHER ANIMALS BREATHE IN OXYGEN (WHICH THE BODY USES TO CONVERT FOOD INTO ENERGY) AND BREATHE OUT CARBON DIOXIDE.

PLANTS TAKE IN CARBON DIOXIDE AND CONVERT IT INTO BOTH FOOD (BY PHOTOSYNTHESIS) AND THE PLANT ITSELF. PLANTS THEN GIVE OUT OXYGEN.

OXYGEN →  → CARBON DIOXIDE   CARBON DIOXIDE → → OXYGEN

Atmospheric layers

Scientists split the atmosphere into five main layers.

1 TROPOSPHERE (0–6 MI) = WEATHER OCCURS HERE. CONTAINS MOST OF THE ATMOSPHERIC GASES. HELICOPTERS FLY BELOW 1.6 MI.

2 STRATOSPHERE (6–31 MI) = CONTAINS A LAYER OF GAS CALLED OZONE, WHICH PROTECTS EARTH FROM HARMFUL RAYS. AIRCRAFT FLY HERE.

3 MESOSPHERE (31–50 MI) = VERY COLD. FALLING METEORITES BURN UP IN THIS LAYER. WEATHER BALLOONS FOUND UP TO 31 MI.

4 THERMOSPHERE (50–311 MI) = AS HOT AS 3,632°F. ELECTRICITY IN THE LAYER CREATES THE NORTHERN LIGHTS. SPACE SHUTTLE FLIES HERE.

5 EXOSPHERE (ABOVE 331 MI) = HARDLY ANY AIR. COMMUNICATION SATELLITES ORBIT HERE.

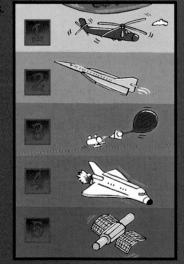

What would Earth be like without an atmosphere?

It would look like the moon, which has no atmosphere:

The surface would be rocky and full of craters.

There would be no oceans, since rain is formed from water vapor in the air.

Temperatures would reach extremes. The days would see fiery highs of 180°F, while the nights would drop to a freezing –220°F.

IN THIS STATE THE PLANET WOULD NOT BE ABLE TO SUPPORT LIFE.

Connect! TURN TO Q42 TO FIND OUT HOW WE ARE SLOWLY LEARNING TO PRESERVE THE CONDITIONS THAT SUPPORT LIFE.

② YOU NEED NOURISHMENT

Everything on the planet depends on the light of the sun. The sun's light is used by plants to make food. Animals eat plants, or other animals, which in turn eat plants. This is called a food chain.

How does a food chain work?

A typical food chain joins together three or four different living things. Each living link in the chain is a source of food for the next one.

  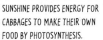 

| SUNSHINE PROVIDES ENERGY FOR CABBAGES TO MAKE THEIR OWN FOOD BY PHOTOSYNTHESIS. | → | CABBAGE LEAVES ARE EATEN BY CATERPILLARS. | → | CATERPILLARS ARE EATEN BY SPARROWS. | → | SPARROWS ARE EATEN BY GOSHAWKS. |

Connect! WERE DINOSAURS KILLED BY A BREAK IN THEIR FOOD CHAIN? SEE Q37.

③ YOU NEED WATER

All plants and animals are made up of water. Almost two-thirds of our bodies consist of water.

WHY DO OUR BODIES NEED WATER TO SURVIVE?

✔ IT ALLOWS CHEMICAL REACTIONS TO TAKE PLACE.

✔ IT COOLS US DOWN.

✔ IT CARRIES NUTRIENTS AROUND THE BODY.

✔ IT DISSOLVES MANY SUBSTANCES.

We need to constantly replace the water lost each day by breathing, sweating, and going to the toilet. Without water, we would die in as few as five days.

Connect! WHAT HAPPENS WHEN RAINWATER TURNS ACIDIC? TURN TO Q39.

④ YOU NEED WARMTH

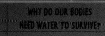

The distance between Earth and the sun is 93 million mi. If Earth was closer to the sun it would be hotter. If it was farther away, it would be cooler. The surface temperature of the sun itself is around 10,830°F.

How does the sun affect the weather?

THE SUN HEATS THE AIR. IT RISES AND LETS COLD AIR MOVE IN. WINDS ARE CREATED IN THE PROCESS.

THE SUN HEATS THE WATER. IT EVAPORATES AND FORMS CLOUDS. WHEN THEY COOL THEY PRODUCE RAIN.

Prove It!

QUESTION

29

How has life on Earth changed since the beginning of time?

AND HOW DOES THIS LINK IN WITH THE LOOK OF THE PLANET?

MYA = MILLION YEARS AGO

Earth was formed about 4.6 billion years ago. The first living cells probably appeared in the oceans 1 billion years later. Since then, Earth and its life-forms have changed in many ways. Take a look at the chart below.

EARTH IS FORMED. IT IS COVERED IN ERUPTING VOLCANOES (4,600 MYA).

PLANET COOLS DOWN AND PRODUCES WATER VAPOR. THIS CONDENSES INTO RAIN, CREATING SEAS AND OCEANS (3,800 MYA).

BACTERIA AND SINGLE-CELLED ALGAE PLANTS ARE FIRST LIFE-FORMS TO APPEAR (3,500 MYA).

TECTONIC PLATE ACTION CREATES LARGE CONTINENTS (2,400 MYA).

LARGER ALGAE PLANTS DEVELOP (1,000 MYA).

FIRST CREATURES ARE WATER-LIVING WORMS AND JELLYFISH. THE OXYGEN IN THE WATER ALLOWS THEM TO SURVIVE (700 MYA).

ANIMALS WITH SHELLS, SUCH AS TRILOBITES, APPEAR IN THE WATER (570-505 MYA).

NO CREATURES ON LAND (570-505 MYA).

THE CONTINENTS ARE FLOODED (505-438 MYA).

GIANT SEA SCORPIONS AND SHELLFISH APPEAR (505-438 MYA).

STILL NO LIFE ON THE LAND (505-438 MYA).

APPEARANCE OF MOLLUSKS, SUCH AS WATER SNAILS AND OYSTERS (438-408 MYA).

ARMORED FISH ARE FIRST CREATURES WITH BACKBONES (438-408 MYA).

FIRST LAND PLANTS, SUCH AS MOSSES AND COOKSONIA, START TO GROW (438-408 MYA).

CORAL REEFS ARE FORMED (408-360 MYA).

DRAGONFLIES, MILLIPEDES, AND OTHER INSECTS APPEAR ON LAND (408-360 MYA).

A TYPE OF FISH CALLED LUNGFISH FLOURISHES IN MURKY, STAGNANT POOLS. THESE FISH DEVELOP LUNGS TO ALLOW THEM TO BREATHE AIR OUT OF THE WATER (408-360 MYA).

SOME AIR-BREATHING FISH START TO COME ASHORE. THEY EVOLVE INTO THE FIRST AMPHIBIANS, SUCH AS HYNERPETON, AND ARE ABLE TO LIVE IN THE WATER AND ON THE LAND (360-286 MYA).

FORESTS OF TREE FERNS AND GIANT HORSETAILS COVER THE LAND (360-286 MYA).

EARLY SHARKS SWIM IN THE OCEANS (360-286 MYA).

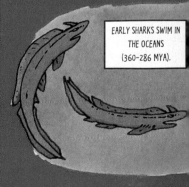

PRECAMBRIAN

PALEOZOIC

4,600 MYA | 570 MYA **CAMBRIAN** | 505 MYA **ORDOVICIAN** | 438 MYA **SILURIAN** | 408 MYA **DEVONIAN** | 360 MYA **CARBONIFEROUS**

Scientists divide Earth's historical time into sections.

1. There are four large segments of time called ERAS.
2. Eras are split into smaller sections called PERIODS.
3. Periods are broken down into EPOCHS.

THE GEOLOGICAL TIMESCALE

KEY

ERA

PERIOD

EPOCH

PRECAMBRIAN	PALEOZOIC						MESOZOIC			CENOZOIC	
	CAMBRIAN	ORDOVICIAN	SILURIAN	DEVONIAN	CARBONIFEROUS	PERMIAN	TRIASSIC	JURASSIC	CRETACEOUS	TERTIARY	QUATERNARY

PALEOCENE EPOCH 65 MYA
EOCENE EPOCH 55 MYA
OLIGOCENE EPOCH 40 MYA
MIOCENE EPOCH 25 MYA
PLIOCENE EPOCH 5 MYA
PLEISTOCENE EPOCH 2 MYA
HOLOCENE EPOCH 0.01 MYA

MILLIONS OF YEARS AGO (MYA)

4,600 MYA
570 MYA
505 MYA
438 MYA
408 MYA
360 MYA
286 MYA
248 MYA
208 MYA
144 MYA
65 MYA
2 MYA
TODAY

THE CONTINENTS JOIN TOGETHER TO FORM THE SUPERCONTINENT PANGAEA (286–248 MYA).

APPEARANCE OF FIRST CONIFER TREES. THE INCREASING LAND VEGETATION PRODUCES LIFE-SUPPORTING OXYGEN IN THE AIR (286–248 MYA).

EARLY MAMMAL-LIKE REPTILES APPEAR. THEY ARE PERFECTLY SUITED TO LIFE ON LAND. THEY DO NOT NEED MUCH WATER TO SURVIVE AND THEIR SCALY SKIN STOPS THEM LOSING BODY WATER (286–248 MYA).

A MASS EXTINCTION AT THE END OF THE PERMIAN ALLOWS MORE COMPLEX REPTILES TO EVOLVE. THESE INCLUDE THE FIRST DINOSAURS (248–213 MYA).

PANGAEA STARTS TO BREAK UP. MUCH OF THE LAND IS DESERT (213–144 MYA).

DINOSAURS DEVELOP INTO ALL SHAPES AND SIZES AND RULE THE PLANET (213–144 MYA).

THE FIRST BIRDS, SUCH AS ARCHAEOPTERYX, EVOLVE FROM THE SMALLER DINOSAURS. THEY TAKE TO THE SKIES, WHERE THERE IS LESS CHANCE OF BEING KILLED (213–144 MYA).

PLANTS WITH FLOWERS START TO BLOOM ON LAND (144–65 MYA).

SMALL MAMMALS APPEAR, SUCH AS CRUSAFONTIA AND HENKELOTHERIUM (144–65 MYA).

TOWARD THE END OF THE PERIOD, THE DINOSAURS AND MANY OTHER ANIMALS BECOME EXTINCT. ONE THEORY IS THAT THEY ARE UNABLE TO ADAPT TO EARTH'S CHANGING CLIMATE, WHICH IS BECOMING MORE SEASONAL AND LESS TROPICAL (144–65 MYA).

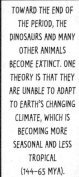

PANGAEA SPLITS UP INTO SEPARATE CONTINENTS (144–65 MYA).

COLLIDING CONTINENTS FORM ROCKY MOUNTAINS AND THE HIMALAYAS (65–2 MYA).

COLORADO RIVER CARVES OUT THE GRAND CANYON (65–2 MYA).

THE GAP LEFT BY THE DEATH OF THE DINOSAURS ALLOWS BIRDS AND MAMMALS TO TAKE OVER AND SPREAD (65–2 MYA).

EARLY COWS, HORSES, PIGS, AND ELEPHANTS APPEAR (65–2 MYA).

NORTH AND SOUTH AMERICA JOIN TOGETHER (2 MYA).

EARLY HUMANS APPEAR. THEY HAVE THICK SKINS, HEAVY BONES, AND FURRY BODIES TO PROTECT THEM FROM THE COLD (1.8 MYA).

Connect!

HUMANS HAVE ONLY BEEN AROUND FOR A SHORT TIME. TURN TO Q39 TO SEE HOW THEY HAVE POLLUTED THE PLANET.

AGRICULTURE BEGINS (10,000 YEARS AGO).

Connect!

WHAT IS THE FUTURE OF LIFE ON EARTH? SEE Q41.

MESOZOIC

CENOZOIC

| 286 MYA **PERMIAN** | 248 MYA **TRIASSIC** | 208 MYA **JURASSIC** | 144 MYA **CRETACEOUS** | 65 MYA **TERTIARY** | 2 MYA **QUATERNARY** |

TODAY

30 How do we know what was living on Earth in the past?

By looking at rocks, fossils, and other geographical clues, scientists and geologists are able to piece together the history of life on Earth.

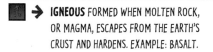
Looking at rocks

Geologists look at the characteristics of rocks to tell them how and where they were formed. Radioactive dating measures the radiation in the rocks to calculate their age.

☆ THERE ARE THREE KINDS OF ROCKS

1 → **IGNEOUS** FORMED WHEN MOLTEN ROCK, OR MAGMA, ESCAPES FROM THE EARTH'S CRUST AND HARDENS. EXAMPLE: BASALT. →

2 → **SEDIMENTARY** LAID DOWN IN LAYERS, OR STRATA, AND FORMED FROM OTHER ROCK FRAGMENTS, OR SEDIMENTS, WHICH ARE SQUEEZED TOGETHER. EXAMPLE: SANDSTONE. →

3 → **METAMORPHIC** IGNEOUS AND SEDIMENTARY ROCKS THAT HAVE BEEN CHANGED BY HEAT AND/OR PRESSURE. EXAMPLE: MARBLE. →

☆ WHAT DOES THE ROCK LAYER TELL US?

Layers of rock are laid down on top of each other. If they haven't been disturbed, the bottom layer will be the oldest. The layers above are all from more recent periods of time.

← **SANDSTONE** THIS IS THE TOP LAYER AND THE YOUNGEST. IT SUGGESTS A DESERT AREA.

← **COAL** MAINLY APPEARED IN THE CARBONIFEROUS PERIOD, WHEN COAL-FORMING FORESTS THRIVED, ABOUT 320 MILLION YEARS AGO.

← **SHALE** FORMED FROM RIVER MUD, SO THE LAND AT THIS TIME MUST HAVE BEEN UNDER WATER.

← **BASALT** BOTTOM LAYER, THEREFORE THE OLDEST. BASALT IS FORMED FROM LAVA, SO THIS LAYER WAS CREATED BY AN ERUPTING VOLCANO.

CAN YOU SEE WHAT HAS HAPPENED TO THE LAND OVER TIME?

Connect! HUMANS ARE OBSESSED WITH FINDING OUT MORE ABOUT THE PLANET AND LIFE ON EARTH. FIND OUT MORE IN Q31.

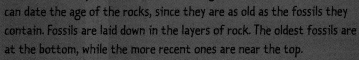
Looking at fossils

Sedimentary rocks often contain fossils – the remains of dead plants and animals. Geologists can date the age of the rocks, since they are as old as the fossils they contain. Fossils are laid down in the layers of rock. The oldest fossils are at the bottom, while the more recent ones are near the top.

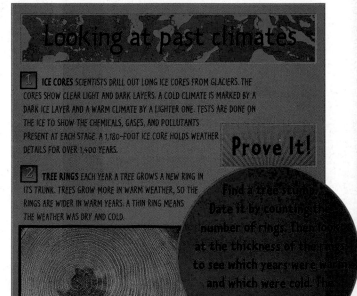

Looking at past climates

1 **ICE CORES** SCIENTISTS DRILL OUT LONG ICE CORES FROM GLACIERS. THE CORES SHOW CLEAR LIGHT AND DARK LAYERS. A COLD CLIMATE IS MARKED BY A DARK ICE LAYER AND A WARM CLIMATE BY A LIGHTER ONE. TESTS ARE DONE ON THE ICE TO SHOW THE CHEMICALS, GASES, AND POLLUTANTS PRESENT AT EACH STAGE. A 1,180-FOOT ICE CORE HOLDS WEATHER DETAILS FOR OVER 1,400 YEARS.

2 **TREE RINGS** EACH YEAR A TREE GROWS A NEW RING IN ITS TRUNK. TREES GROW MORE IN WARM WEATHER, SO THE RINGS ARE WIDER IN WARM YEARS. A THIN RING MEANS THE WEATHER WAS DRY AND COLD.

Prove It!

Find a tree stump. Date it by counting the number of rings. Then look at the thickness of the rings to see which years were warm and which were cold. The ring nearest the bark is the most recent.

It's time to look at the

future

What future?

How are humans learning to control the planet?

What is the future of life on Earth?

Is there anywhere left to be discovered?

Take a look at the future of the planet in this final part of your journey. Just turn the page and move onto PART FOUR. ----✈

QUESTION

31 Why do humans explore the planet?

Apart from being naturally curious, there are many reasons why past explorers searched out new lands. Study the list on the right.

FOR INQUISITIVE PEOPLE EMBARKING ON GREAT ADVENTURES.

FOR FARMERS AND WORKERS LOOKING FOR BETTER LAND AND WORK OPPORTUNITIES.

FOR PEOPLE SEARCHING FOR TREASURE AND OTHER RICHES, SUCH AS GOLD AND OIL.

FOR MERCHANTS LOOKING FOR NEW TRADE ROUTES AND SUPPLIES OF GOODS.

FOR MISSIONARIES CONVERTING OTHER PEOPLES TO THEIR OWN RELIGION.

☆ EXPLORING OUR SURROUNDINGS HELPS US TO UNDERSTAND THE WAY THE EARTH IS STRUCTURED.

Have people always pictured the world as we do today?

No! Although we know the world is round, early civilizations did not see it that way. There were no accurate maps and most people thought the world was flat. They believed that if they traveled far enough they would drop off the edge of the earth into black space.

SOME PEOPLE THOUGHT THE WORLD WAS SUPPORTED BY FOUR ELEPHANTS WALKING ON TOP OF A GIANT TORTOISE.

Proving that the earth was not flat

WHEN?	WHO?	WHERE?	
1271–96	MARCO POLO	HE JOURNEYS THROUGH ASIA.	
1492–93	CHRISTOPHER COLUMBUS	HE EXPLORES THE WEST INDIES.	
1497–98	VASCO DA GAMA	HE DISCOVERS THE SEA ROUTE FROM EUROPE TO INDIA.	
1519–22	FERDINAND MAGELLAN	LEADER OF FIRST EUROPEAN EXPEDITION TO SAIL AROUND THE WORLD.	

Connect!

TURN TO Q34 TO SEE WHAT THE FIRST MAPS LOOKED LIKE.

Journeys to the unknown

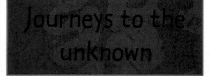

EXPLORING THE OCEANS FIRST STUDIED PROPERLY IN 1872 BY HMS CHALLENGER. THE OCEAN FLOORS WERE NOT EXPLORED UNTIL OVER 70 YEARS LATER. TODAY, REMOTE-CONTROLLED UNDERWATER VEHICLES AND SUBMERSIBLES ALLOW SCIENTISTS TO DESCEND TO GREATER DEPTHS.

EXPLORING THE ANTARCTIC THIS FROZEN WINTERLAND HAS ONLY BEEN EXPLORED QUITE RECENTLY. IN 1958, THE BRITISH COMMONWEALTH TRANS-ANTARCTIC EXPEDITION BECAME THE FIRST SCIENTIFIC MISSION TO REACH THE SOUTH POLE.

QUESTION

What is there left to be discovered?

From steamy jungles and dangerous mountains, to arid deserts and deep oceans, people have explored almost every corner of the globe. This has been possible because of major advances in modern technology and transportation. But there are still a few places we know little about.

THE DARKEST AND DEEPEST POINTS IN THE OCEANS, WHERE NEW ANIMAL SPECIES ARE STILL BEING DISCOVERED.

MOUNTAINOUS REGIONS, WHERE UNCONFIRMED REPORTS OF STRANGE ANIMALS, SUCH AS THE YETI, ARE COMMON.

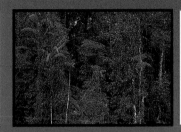

THE THICKER, DENSER PARTS OF RAIN FORESTS, PARTICULARLY IN THE FOLIAGE ABOVE THE FOREST FLOOR.

Connect! HOW DOES DESTROYING THE RAIN FORESTS AFFECT THE REST OF THE PLANET? SEE Q44.

QUESTION

How have people learned to control the planet?

SURVIVING ON THE PLANET

People have made their homes in some of the world's most hostile environments. Increased knowledge means that people can survive in almost any conditions.

CONDITION	SOLUTION	EXAMPLE	
TOO HOT	ELECTRIC FANS AND AIR CONDITIONING.	IT MAY BE 95°F OUTSIDE A HOTEL IN INDIA, BUT INSIDE IT'S A COOL 50°F.	
TOO COLD	HEATING AND INSULATION.	A HOUSE IN GREENLAND IS KEPT WARM BY LOG AND GAS FIRES.	
TOO WET	DRAINAGE AND RAISED BUILDINGS.	INDONESIAN VILLAGES ARE BUILT ON STILTS TO PROTECT THEM FROM FLOODS.	
TOO DRY	IRRIGATION.	WATER CHANNELED FROM DAMS OR RIVERS TURNS DESERTS INTO GREEN FARMLAND.	

CHANGING THE NATURAL WORLD

Humans started plowing, irrigating, mining, and grazing the land around 10,000 years ago. Only 15% of the earth's land surface remains untouched. The rest has been changed and shaped to suit our needs.

THE NETHERLANDS IS CONSTANTLY UNDER THREAT FROM THE SEA. IN THE MIDDLE AGES NEARLY A THIRD OF THE LAND WAS INVADED BY WATER. IT WAS RECLAIMED BY BUILDING DYKES (LONG WALLS) AND DRAINING THE LAND.

HARNESSING NATURAL RESOURCES

WATER Although water is necessary for life, it can also be deadly. Too little causes droughts and too much causes floods. How do we control such a powerful resource?

DAMS ARE LARGE WATER BARRIERS. THEY WORK BY:
● STORING WATER IN A RESERVOIR. THE WATER SUPPLY CAN THEN BE CONTROLLED THROUGHOUT THE YEAR.
● HOLDING BACK WATER. THIS PREVENTS FLOODING. THE WATER IN THE RESERVOIR CAN ALSO PROVIDE ENERGY, BY DRIVING TURBINES TO GENERATE ELECTRICITY.

FUELS Other natural resources used by people include: coal, oil, natural gas, and wood.

Connect! WHAT EFFECT CAN USING UP THE EARTH'S RESOURCES HAVE ON THE PLANET? TURN TO Q39.

25

34 Why do we need maps?

Maps help us to understand our surroundings. Without them, we would not know what the rest of our town, country, or world looked like.

● Cavemen were probably the first mapmakers. They painted scenes showing themselves hunting and sometimes included details such as the trees and rocks they found along the way.

● Maps as we know them appeared much later. The oldest on record is a clay tablet dating back to 3800 B.C. It shows the Euphrates River flowing through northern Mesopotamia, Iraq.

EARLY MAPS

700 B.C. BABYLONIAN CLAY MAP SHOWS THE KNOWN WORLD AT THAT TIME – MESOPOTAMIA AND THE SEA.

A.D. 50 ROMAN MAPMAKER POMPONIUS MELA GETS AFRICA AND THE AMERICAS BADLY WRONG.

A.D. 1076 IN THIS FRENCH MAP, THE BIBLICAL GARDEN OF EDEN APPEARS IN THE EAST, NEAR INDIA.

35 Why are maps drawn as they are?

Maps can be drawn in many different styles, each highlighting different information about a place. Take a look below at the three main types of map.

1 **GENERAL REFERENCE** maps show a number of geographical features, such as mountains, rivers, land boundaries, towns, cities, and roads.

2 **MOBILITY** maps show how to get from one place to another, as in road and street maps.

3 **THEMATIC** maps highlight a certain feature, or several features, such as population, rainfall, or oilfields.

Prove It!

Draw a general reference map of your neighborhood. Then draw a mobility map of the streets. Finally, make a thematic map showing a feature such as stores, parks, or TV satellite dishes.

36 Why do maps change?

The planet is constantly changing. Countries and cities change their names, new borders appear, rivers alter their courses, and oceans wear away coastlines. Maps need to be redrawn regularly if they are to be up-to-date.

IN THE 1970S, MAPMAKER RICHARD CIACCI DREW AN IMAGINARY MOUNTAIN ON MAPS OF COLORADO. IT WAS TWO YEARS BEFORE ANYONE NOTICED THE FAKE MOUNT RICHARD!

IN 1963, A NEW ISLAND CALLED SURTSEY ROSE FROM THE ICELANDIC SEA. IT WAS CREATED BY AN ERUPTING UNDERWATER VOLCANO.

FOR SECURITY REASONS, THE RUSSIAN TOWN OF LOGASHKINO DISAPPEARED FROM MAPS FOR 15 YEARS, FROM 1954.

☆ DO WE ALL SEE THE WORLD IN THE SAME WAY?

COUNTRIES OFTEN PRODUCE MAPS WHICH PUT THEIR OWN AREA IN THE CENTER OF THE PICTURE.

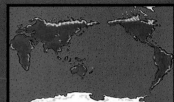

FOR EUROPEANS AND AMERICANS, AFRICA AND ASIA ARE FAR-OFF LANDS.

CHINESE PEOPLE VIEW THE WORLD AS CENTERED AROUND THE PACIFIC AND INDIAN OCEANS.

37 Have humans always dominated other life-forms?

No. The different stages of evolution mean that various groups of animals have ruled supreme at different times.

38 Why did humans become dominant?

Humans are not the biggest mammals, nor are they the strongest. So what made them rule over everything else?

DINOSAURS

This vast group of reptiles was once the dominant life-form on the planet. They reigned for 160 million years. Part of their success was that they had longer legs than other reptiles, which enabled them to move fast. Scientists still do not know why dinosaurs died out. One theory is that their food chain was affected. It is thought a comet crashed into the earth, sending out huge dust clouds that covered the sun. Plants died because they needed the sun to make their food. First plant-eating and then meat-eating dinosaurs starved to death.

GIANT BIRDS

The world would have been very different if mammals had not become dominant. Evidence suggests that in New Zealand giant birds would have risen to the top. This is because New Zealand is an island that most mammals could not reach because of the sea, but birds and insects had no problem flying to. Gradually, big birds such as moas and ostriches evolved because there was little competition from mammals. And for a while, when the dinosaurs became extinct and mammals were quite small., birds became big and dominant.

MAMMALS

When dinosaurs died out mammals began to flourish. Previously they had been small. Now they started to grow bigger and develop into hundreds of new species. A big effect on their evolution came from the separation of the continents. Distinct groups appeared on each landmass, from the kangaroos of Australia to the elephants of India and Asia. This buildup of natural power centers has allowed mammals to become the dominant land animals for the past 65 million years.

◯ LARGE BRAIN AND HIGH INTELLIGENCE.
◯ ABILITY TO MAKE TOOLS FOR SURVIVAL.
◯ ABILITY TO WORK AND COOPERATE WITH OTHERS.
◯ FEW NATURAL PREDATORS.
◯ ABILITY TO SPEAK AND COMMUNICATE
◯ ABILITY TO USE CLOTHES, BUILDINGS, AND TRANSPORTATION TO ADAPT TO A VERY LARGE RANGE OF ENVIRONMENTS.

Connect!

SEE Q41 TO FIND OUT HOW HUMANS ADAPT TO A DECAYING WORLD.

How have people damaged the planet?

Earth is the only planet in our solar system known to support life. Humans have successfully colonized the land – but at a cost. We are steadily damaging the very conditions that allow life to exist on the planet. How?

THE WAY WE LIVE

OUR DAY-TO-DAY ACTIONS ARE AFFECTING THE ENVIRONMENT. GLOBAL WARMING, DESTRUCTION OF THE OZONE LAYER, AND ACID RAIN ARE JUST SOME OF THE WAYS WE ARE DESTROYING THE EARTH.

1 POLLUTION

MORE THAN ONE-FIFTH OF THE WORLD'S POPULATION BREATHES IN POLLUTED AIR.

THE POLLUTANTS COME FROM MANY SOURCES:
CAR EXHAUST FUMES.
FACTORIES BELCHING OUT SMOKE.
SMOKE FROM BURNING FORESTS.
POWER STATIONS PRODUCING CARBON DIOXIDE GAS.
AEROSOLS.
THE INCINERATION OF WASTE, PRODUCING CARBON DIOXIDE GAS.

BAD NEWS BECAUSE... → POLLUTION CAUSES BREATHING DIFFICULTIES AND DESTROYS VEGETATION.

2 THE OZONE LAYER DESTROYED

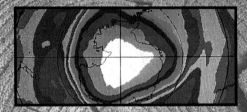

SOME AEROSOLS AND REFRIGERATORS CONTAIN CHEMICALS CALLED CHLOROFLUOROCARBONS (CFCS). WHEN RELEASED INTO THE AIR, CFCS DESTROY THE OZONE LAYER, WHICH PROTECTS US FROM THE SUN'S HARMFUL ULTRAVIOLET RAYS.

BAD NEWS BECAUSE... → A BREAKDOWN IN THE OZONE LAYER CAUSES MORE SKIN CANCER AND BLINDNESS IN HUMANS.

3 THE GREENHOUSE EFFECT

THE EARTH'S NATURAL LAYER OF GASES ACTS LIKE A GREENHOUSE. IT LETS IN HEAT, THEN PREVENTS IT FROM LEAVING. THIS IS KNOWN AS THE GREENHOUSE EFFECT. HOWEVER, THE GREENHOUSE GASES, SUCH AS CFCS AND CARBON DIOXIDE, ARE BUILDING UP. MORE HEAT IS BEING TRAPPED, LEADING TO AN INCREASE IN TEMPERATURE, CALLED GLOBAL WARMING.

BAD NEWS BECAUSE... → THE GREENHOUSE EFFECT CAUSES SEA LEVELS TO RISE AND FLOOD LOW-LYING LAND.

Connect!

IS GLOBAL WARMING A REAL THREAT? TURN TO Q45.

4 ACID RAIN

BURNING FOSSIL FUELS, SUCH AS COAL AND OIL, RELEASES GASES CONTAINING SULFUR AND NITROGEN INTO THE AIR. THE GASES COMBINE WITH WATER DROPLETS, TURNING THEM SLIGHTLY ACIDIC. THEY FALL TO EARTH AS ACID RAIN.

BAD NEWS BECAUSE... → ACID RAIN KILLS TREES AND WILDLIFE AND DESTROYS BUILDINGS.

Prove It!

Acid rain eats away at statues and buildings. Tree leaves die and the rings in tree trunks grow very close together. Which of these signs can you spot in your area?

HOW DO OUR ACTIONS AFFECT PLANTS AND ANIMALS?

HUMAN POLLUTION HAS AN EFFECT ON PLANTS AND ANIMALS. THEIR NATURAL COMMUNITIES, OR **ECOSYSTEMS**, CAN BREAK DOWN.

1. ACID RAIN FALLS INTO LAKE.

2. MERCURY, ALUMINUM, AND LEAD LEVELS IN THE WATER INCREASE. THIS DECREASES THE AMOUNT OF OXYGEN FISH CAN ABSORB.

3. FISH DIE AND UPSET THE FOOD CHAIN. ONLY SMALL CREATURES SURVIVE.

QUESTION

40 How recently has this damage been done?

Suppose all the time since the birth of Earth was squeezed into one year...

THE EARTH WAS BORN ON JANUARY 1. → → THE EARLIEST HUMANS APPEARED AT 6:15 P.M. ON DECEMBER 31. →

IN VERY LITTLE TIME HUMANS HAVE DAMAGED THE PLANET LIKE NO SPECIES BEFORE THEM.

How?

THE MAIN DEMANDS ON THE EARTH'S LAND, ENERGY, AND RESOURCES HAVE BEEN:

1. → **THE AGRICULTURAL REVOLUTION** THIS BEGAN 10,000 YEARS AGO. IT LED TO MASS FARMING AND LAND CULTIVATION.

2. → **THE INDUSTRIAL REVOLUTION** THIS BEGAN IN ABOUT 1760. FACTORIES, MILLS, AND LARGE MACHINERY USED LOTS OF FUEL AND PRODUCED POLLUTING FUMES.

3. → **THE POPULATION EXPLOSION** UNTIL 1830, THE WORLD POPULATION WAS ABOUT 1 BILLION. THE NEXT 100 YEARS SAW THIS FIGURE DOUBLE. BY THE YEAR 2000, EXPERTS BELIEVE IT MAY REACH 6 BILLION.

WARS AND CONFLICTS HAVE DEVASTATING EFFECTS ON TOWNS AND COUNTRIES.

IN 1945, AN ATOM BOMB COMPLETELY WIPED OUT THE JAPANESE CITY OF HIROSHIMA. THE EXPLOSION DESTROYED 90,000 BUILDINGS AND FLATTENED EVERYTHING IN SIGHT.

THE GULF WAR IN 1991 CAUSED THE WORLD'S LARGEST OIL SPILL – EIGHT MILLION BARRELS ENTERED THE SEA. AROUND 700 OIL WELLS WERE SET ON FIRE, CREATING SERIOUS AIR POLLUTION.

QUESTION

41 What is the future of life on Earth?

The evolution of the human race depends on the way it adapts to the environment. If we are not to become extinct, we need to cope with the modern problems of industrialization, pollution, and urban living.

Connect! TURN TO Q44 TO FIND OUT THE PROBLEMS FACED BY POORER COUNTRIES.

↑ Is this our future? A Japanese tourist in Florence, Italy, wears a smog mask to protect herself from the growing air pollution.

HOW DOES THE ENVIRONMENT'S STATE AFFECT LIFE ON EARTH?

IN 19TH CENTURY NORTHERN ENGLAND, THE PEPPERED MOTH QUICKLY ADAPTED TO COPE WITH ITS NEW, SMOKY SURROUNDINGS.

Before 1850s Light-colored moths thrived as they were camouflaged by light-colored tree trunks.

1850s Pollution from factories turned the trunks black. Birds easily spotted the pale moths and ate them. The naturally darker moths were now perfectly camouflaged to survive, and they produced darker offspring.

1900s Darker-colored moths flourished.

What can we do to save the planet?

In a short space of time we have created an enormous amount of pollution and over-used the earth's resources. But it is not too late to change the situation.

We must learn to meet our needs in ways that won't spoil future generations' chances of meeting their needs. This is known as **sustainable development**. How can we achieve this state?

Every day we make choices, some of which can help to save the planet.

☆ WHAT WE THROW AWAY

In the natural world, nothing is wasted. Everything breaks down naturally, or biodegrades. Waste produced by humans and buried in landfill sites does not always biodegrade and can release poisons into the soil.

- REUSE AND MEND AS MANY THINGS AS YOU CAN.
- RECYCLE ALL PAPER, BOTTLES, CANS, AND PLASTICS.

☆ HOW WE TRAVEL

New road systems destroy the land they run through. The topsoil is removed and trees and plants are uprooted. Changing the environment in this way kills the area's ecosystems. Cars pollute the atmosphere by releasing greenhouse gases.

- WHERE POSSIBLE, WALK, BIKE, OR USE PUBLIC TRANSPORTATION.
- CARS SHOULD USE UNLEADED GAS AND BE FITTED WITH CATALYTIC CONVERTERS TO REDUCE EXHAUST FUMES.

Prove It!

☆ HOW WE RUN INDUSTRY

Fossil fuels such as coal, oil, and gas will eventually run out. They also produce harmful greenhouse gases when burned. Scientists are looking at alternative forms of fuel that are clean and that never run out.

WATER IN ARIZONA, IN THE USA, THE GLEN CANYON DAM MAKES ENERGY BY USING TIDAL AND WAVE POWER.

WIND THE TURBINES ON THIS WIND FARM SUPPLY ENOUGH ELECTRICITY FOR A SMALL TOWN.

☆ WHAT WE BUY

Public pressure can make stores sell products that are kinder to the environment. Shoppers complained about aerosols containing ozone-destroying CFCs, so manufacturers made new aerosols that did not use them.

- BUY ECOPRODUCTS, WHICH DO NOT DAMAGE THE ENVIRONMENT.
- AVOID HEAVILY PACKAGED GOODS. THEY COST MORE AND CREATE A LOT OF WASTE.

SUN THIS SOLAR POWER STATION PRODUCES ELECTRICITY BY COLLECTING HEAT AND LIGHT ENERGY FROM THE SUN.

Connect! WHERE IS THE PLANET HEADING? SEE Q45.

43 What are world leaders doing?

Governments around the world hold special meetings, or summits, to talk about the situation. They look at ways of stopping the destruction of the planet.

 HOW?

1  **CONSERVATION** LOOKING AFTER AND PRESERVING ANIMAL AND PLANT LIFE.

2 **FUNDING** GIVING MONEY FOR RESEARCH AND ENVIRONMENTAL PROJECTS.

3  **EDUCATION** MAKING SURE PEOPLE AND INDUSTRY ARE AWARE OF THE PROBLEMS AND KNOW WHAT MUST BE DONE.

QUESTION

44 What is happening in developing countries?

People in developing countries often find themselves in no-choice situations.

Many people live in poverty and survive by working the land. The problem is that much of the land is of poor quality. An estimated 500 million people live and farm on land facing serious erosion.

EVERY YEAR:
- 42 MILLION ACRES OF TROPICAL FORESTS ARE DESTROYED.
- 15 MILLION ACRES OF DRY LAND TURNS TO DUST.
- BILLIONS OF TONS OF TOPSOIL ARE WASHED AND BLOWN AWAY.

Families have little choice but to cultivate the land. Soon it becomes useless for growing anything at all. The family either starves or moves to a new area, where the same thing happens again.

QUESTION

45 What is the future of the planet?

Global warming is perhaps the biggest threat to the planet. If we continue to damage Earth, by the year 2050 temperatures may have risen by as much as 10°F. This will have striking effects on the world's climates.

POLAR ICE CAPS WILL MELT.

SEA LEVELS WILL RISE BY AT LEAST 1.6 FT.

COASTAL AREAS WILL BECOME FLOODED AND ISLANDS DISAPPEAR.

DESERTS WILL SPREAD IN THE U.S., AFRICA, AND EUROPE.

HURRICANES WILL INCREASE IN THE GULF OF MEXICO.

Connections!

Remember, the results of our actions on the Earth will be passed onto all future generations. If we continue to destroy the planet, it will end up destroying us. ●

Connections!
EARTH
Index

☆ **PICTURE CREDITS** P1 Science Photo Library. P3 Science Photo Library. P4 left: World Pictures; right: Science Photo Library. P5 Science Photo Library. P6 top left, top right: World Pictures; panel: Science Photo Library. P7 Science Photo Library. P8 panel: Science Photo Library; left: Britstock – IFA; center: The Hutchinson Library; right: Art Directions. P9 top: Ident file; bottom: World Pictures. P10 panel: Science Photo Library. P11 panel: Popperfoto. P12 panel: Science Photo Library; right: The Image Bank. P13 panel: Popperfoto; far left, center left: Still Pictures; center right: World Pictures; far right: Robert Francis. P15 top: Art Directors; bottom: Science Photo Library. P16 top, bottom, panel: Science Photo Library. P17 top left, top right: Bruce Coleman; bottom left, bottom right, far right: Ace. P19 panel left: Popperfoto; panel right, top, bottom: Science Photo Library. P20 Science Photo Library. P21 Science Photo Library. P22 left top, left center, left bottom, bottom: GSF Picture Library; right: Science Photo Library. P23 left, right: Still Pictures. P24 panel: Britstock – IFA; right top: Science Photo Library; right bottom: Royal Geographical Society. P25 top left: Pictures International; top center: Royal Geographical Society; top right, bottom left, bottom right: Still Pictures. P26 left: Ancient Art + Architecture Collection; center: May Evans Picture Library; right: AKG London. P27 Ace. P28 left, bottom: Still Pictures; center, panel: Science Photo Library. P29 top left, top right: Science Photo Library; bottom: Hutchinson Library. P30 top left: Britstock – IFA; top right: Rex Features; center top, bottom right, far left: Science Photo Library; centerbottom: Hutchinson Library; bottom left: The Environmental Picture Library. P31 Hutchinson Library.